CW00734973

Southern Verses

Edited by Annabel Cook

Poetry by the People
for the People

anchorbooks

First published in Great Britain in 2007 by:
Anchor Books
Remus House
Coltsfoot Drive
Peterborough
PE2 9JX
Telephone: 01733 898102
Website: www.forwardpress.co.uk

SB ISBN 978-1 84418 468 2

Foreword

Anchor Books is a small press, established in 1992, with the aim of promoting readable poetry to as wide an audience as possible.

We hope to establish an outlet for writers of poetry who may have struggled to see their work in print.

The poems presented here have been selected from many entries, and as always editing proved to be a difficult task.

I trust this selection will delight and please the authors and all those who enjoy reading poetry.

Annabel Cook

Editor

Contents

The Poems

Old Age

Depressed?   Why should I be?
But when you start to think a bit
It's pretty final when you die
And all the things you had before
Very soon you'll have no more.

The things you love,
          The things you hate
Won't matter
          As it's all too late.
Memories and problems gone
          And triumphs and disasters done.

The hospital upon the State
          Is this for me a future date?
MRSA and A&E
          What will they think of next for me?
Old age has crept up on me fast
          While I've been thinking of my past.

What do I think while lying in bed?
          Being flooded out or mugged at home,
And do they not resuscitate
          As this is all my coming fate?
Do I feel the World's gone mad
          Or is it me just feeling sad?

When I was young so long ago
          My parents simply just said, 'No'
And with the teacher at my school
          Never thought me being a fool.

Were they really then the Good Old Days
          Or have we simply changed our ways?
'Help The Aged' that's my cry
          And if they don't, it's 'Do or Die'.

My family live far away
          So will a friend pop in today?
So here I sit and all alone
          Just think and wait.

          Please someone phone.

John Thorpe (Romsey)

Auntie Eileen

The cockerel crows, it's nearly morn
The grass is fresh with dew
The cows are standing by the gate
Auntie Eileen, they are waiting just for you.
By the back gate the fox comes to greet
While busy in her garden
Chickens running up the path
Eileen always feeds them.

The sheep are on a muddy track,
Wagging their tails behind them
My auntie holds them one by one
When she wants to shear them.

So green, so green the fields would be
Before my auntie ploughed them
Then throw the seed on the land
While the birds are waiting close to hand.

Auntie Eileen, I have treasured thoughts
Of you working on the land, it fills my heart with glee
So brave and strong, never did anything wrong
That's my Auntie Eileen.

Madeline Reade (Swindon)

Anchor Books - Southern Verses

Salisbury Cathedral

The cathedral stands tall and great
In the sunshine it stands out
It stands out like a bright light
The spire is so tall you can see it for miles around
When it is dark you can see the light
That shines at the top and guides you wherever you want to go
Through the blackness of the night
The figures on the wall show up in the moonlight
The surrounding countryside shows its true beauty
The beauty is a marvel to see
The stained glass windows are glorious colours
Each window tells a different story
The cathedral is a marvel
And stands out above the rest.

Sarah Langridge (Amesbury)

The Sea Of Brake Lights

Circumstance
I wondered since
The car in front stood still
It was clear
We'd remain here
As we lined up on the hill
Destination
Put on hold
To think I'd be there by now
I didn't heed the warning signs
I see them clearly now

I saw the young man
In his car
Of the kind that's built for speed
Shooting past
The scattered mass
Though he knew there was no need
Jumped a red light
Far too late
Oncoming car spun him out
I never saw him overtake
I see him clearly now

In the aftermath
Came a blinding flash
Of the fire engine's beacon
Stage by stage
Cut the mangled cage
And pulled that man to freedom
Rubberneckers
Worsening matters
Taking a look - slowing down
But they won't know how close they came
They've seen it clearly now.

Martyn Leroy (Swindon)

Bus Stop Fantasy

Waiting at the bus stop
In the early morning queue
I cannot make my mind up
On what I have to do.
Shall I go to work today
Or shall I stay at home?
Extend my world of fantasy
Like, take a trip to Rome?
I could see the Roman ruins
See St Peter's in the square
Even sit around the fountain
Throw some coins in while I'm there.
Or perhaps I'll ring the Pope up
Invite myself to tea
He might give me a blessing
For a small Italian fee.
My train of thought's invaded
I'm back here in the queue
My bus is coming round the bend
I can see the driver too.
So it's just another day, I fear
I wonder, will I get a seat
Or stand up while some lousy swine
Tramples on my feet?
Oh, all right, let's to go work
Don't let things get me down
I'll just get my pay tomorrow
And have a night out on the town.

Ernie Hannam (Rustingdon)

Waste Not, Want Not

Sometimes when I am eating out
They fill my plate so full
I gaze with relish - but I doubt
If I can eat it all.

The food is fine, it isn't that,
I savour every bite
I'm not afraid of getting fat,
It's just my appetite.

A little is enough for me
And halfway through I'm floored,
I have no more capacity
To take the rest on board.

To think they'd throw it all away
It fills my heart with sorrow:
But what I cannot eat today
Why can't I eat tomorrow?

I cannot pocket it all loose -
But with a bright forethought
From my coat pocket I produce
A doggy bag I've brought!

So in a deft and furtive way
My doggy bag I fill:
If I don't fancy it next day
My little pussy will.

Now you may laugh at me, I know,
And think I'm rather queer
But didn't Someone long ago
Have much the same idea?

He fed the hungry multitude
From one lad's fish and bread;
When they had eaten all they could,
'Collect what's left,' He said.

They must have thought it pretty cool,
For when they did obey
They found they had twelve baskets full
To eat another day!

Lynette Nicholson (Crawley)

Perfect

Perfect that, perfect this
Perfect smile, with a kiss
Perfect hair, perfect clothes
Watch perfection as it grows.

In my lies I'll soon be caught
All of this is what I'm not
Not that you all give a damn
But this is who I really am.

Perfect blood, palest skin
Dying outside, dead within
Weakest body that has bled
Perfect screaming in my head
I'm not screwed up like they all say
I'm just perfect in my own way.

Charlotte Kelly (Crawley)

A Week On The Canals 2002

Sleep came slowly to me at night
That night on the Union Canal
The trees so still
The moon so bright
Not even the hoot of an owl.
I twisted and turned
My pillow like rocks
On shutting my eyes
I was passing through locks.
I thought of our journey
Was it four miles or five?
Only ten minutes if -
We'd decided to drive.
But here on our boat
As life drifts along by
Time stands still
Like the moon in the sky.
But, oh I am weary
I snuggle down deep
And before I know it
I've fallen asleep.

Ruth Clarke (Shoreham-by-Sea)

Arundel Park 10K Run

Racehorses unfold out of the mist,
Outlined darkly against the white.
Hooves thundering and thudding hearts;
The morning sun changing the light.

The bobbly chalk path underfoot
Bending round shrubs where pheasants strut;
Mounting with great gasps Target Hill;
The skylark soars and red deer rut.

Over the rim we scramble like
Frothing and foaming wildebeest,
Grabbing at water that revives
Like parched animals at a feast.

High on a wave of sweat and guts
The pack thunders down The Gallops
Past the spooky black secret copse;
Fungi hanging like giant scallops.

The scent of the kill in the wind
As pros pass rookies on the flat.
Ribcages high we tear through the park,
Fast past the castle and cricketer's bat.

Fire of victory in the veins -
As in the High Street the crowds swell -
With winged feet the front runners sprint
Leaving those behind still in hell.

Joan Woolley (Arundel)

If You Were

If you were the sun
I'd be your sky
So you'd look stunning
To whomever passed you by

If you were a moon
I'd be your night
So that you could be the one
Who is shining so bright

If you saw a baby
I'd be its mum
'Cause a new life is amazing
Especially when it's just begun

If you were a fish
I'd be your sea
So that you could swim
To where you wanted to be

If you were a river
I'd be your stream
So that we could always meet
No matter where we'd be

If you were a girl
I'd be your love
As your love is special
'Cause you're sent from up above.

If you were a rainbow
I'd be your rain
So we could comfort each other
And I'd take all your pain.

Chloe Catlin (Goring-by-Sea)

The Wacky Duckling

A duck and a drake lived on a stream
In a beautiful part of the countryside
They lived there happily and contented
And didn't wish to hide.

In the spring they built their nest
And laid a clutch of eggs
And in due course they hatched and produced
A family, sheltering under the hedge.

A nest of yellow balls of fluff
Which, as the days went by
Gradually turned to feathers of brown
Upon these ducklings, paddling by.

Duck and drake were so proud of them
As they followed their parents about
Until one day, they noticed that
There was an odd one out.

The ducklings swam, as ducklings do
Not clumsily or awkward
Except for one, unlike all the rest
He would *insist* on swimming *backwards.*

He appeared to be like all the others
Diving and paddling too,
He seemed quite pleased, as if to say,
'Mum, Dad, look what I can do.'

Do you think this duckling is a dunce
Or lacking brains? No never
As *he* can swim both forward *and* backwards
I think he is rather clever.

Judith Herrington (Billinghurst)

Where I Live

Rabbits ever fearful flee
Or unaware, play merrily
Pheasants cackle in the chaff
It seems sometimes as if they laugh
And then why not?
For they have got
A beautiful place to be
Such as me
Geese are flying overhead
Geese down here are overfed
The fat of the land all around
Wild cats everywhere abound
Foxes in the night silently creep
You'll see them if you're not asleep
Strange and familiar sounds are heard
Of all the animals and birds
Through the night and through the day
Where are words good enough to say
What it feels like to live here
The place I hold so very dear
Looking out upon open fields
Watching the growing, watching the yields
Trees and bushes, fields and sky
All the wildlife, passing by
I love it all so very much
How can you describe something filled with such
Beauty?

Lynda Hughes (Chichester)

My Weeping Willow

You will always find me
Beside my willow tree.
I talk to him for hours,
Through winter and April showers,
Though he listens patiently,
Yet he never answers me.
These are the words I say,
When I visit him each day.
'Neath your shade I look around
Drooping branches sweep the ground,
As I gaze on your massive height,
Through the gaps I see daylight.
On your branches birds are nesting,
In your shelter people resting.
Tiny feet constantly springing,
Prancing birds, happily singing.
Children climbing, often crying,
Over you wings are flying.
Lovers sharing stolen kiss,
In your comfort finding bliss.
What life's secrets you still hold,
A million stories remain untold,
Summer, winter, autumn, spring
Cherished pleasures to all you bring.
As the years pass you by,
Not a soul has heard you cry.
Do you ever shed real tears,
For those forgotten vanished years?
Weeping willow,
Upon your pillow,
Thick with fallen leaves of gold,
Stowed with treasures buried old.
Tell me truly, do you cry?
I feel sure I heard you sigh!

Shula Bailey (East Grinstead)

Family Ties

Life's drizzle descends
Seeping through the holes of youth
Until it settles in dormant pools.

A futile journey explains
How little I have travelled.

Drawn to the inescapable
Tied to the immeasurable
Knowing that the uncomfortable sense
Of belonging will forever remain.

Justine Sheehan (Wallington)

What's In A Name?

When Azor came to build his camp
He kept it well above the damp;
In fact, he built it high upon the hill.
Later, when the Saxon people
Raised a church (without a steeple)
That was where they built it. It's there still!

Then with many a quip and sally
They watched folk build in the valley
And they laughed and treated them with scorn.
Each one with his neighbour gambles
'Soon their hovels will be shambles,
Wait until the rising of the Bourne!'

Sure enough, there'd come a morning
When came true this awful warning
When would come to pass this woeful day
Valley dwellers homeward turning
Find their hearth fires were not burning
All their homes had been washed right away.

Walls of sods and roof of grasses
Vanish as the water passes
Even as the highland people said,
Carried by the waters surly
To that place now known as Purley
Flushed down to the River Wandle's bed.

Meanwhile on the hill the village
Safe from flood (and, likely, pillage!)
Grew and grew before their very eyes.
Caterham Common was diminished
By each house and shop they finished;
Soon the village reached a Township size.

Queen Victoria ruled the nation
When the railway, with its station,
Down from London to the valley came.
Caring not for man or nature
With no sense of nomenclature
It just pinched the nearest village name.

Local folk, true Caterham's breeding,
Find no one will heed their pleading
Argue or debate it as they will.
There should be a restoration
Of their town's true appellation
Leaving off the suffix 'on-the-hill'.

G A Baker (Caterham)

A Bumpy Ride From Side To Side

How far I've come
How far to go
Up and down
Fast and slow
Life has been
Pretty mean
Don't look back
Think serene
I get down
Get back up
Roller coaster
Sums it up
Life's not fair
Try not to care
But one day
It will stop
No more life
I will drop
Had enough
Learnt my way
Time to think
Time to pay
Don't look back
Go to the light
Don't worry
You've won the fight
I'll be back
Round again
Try not to live my life the same.

Claire King (Farnham)

Make The Effort

When you feel a little low, in need of company,
Do as I do, ring your friends, invite them all,
For tea, or better still for supper then,
Prepare a feast for all,
That will cheer you all I'm sure, lonely? Not at all,
You'll soon find life gets better as you all agree,
To meet again and then again, there's nothing like company,
So make the first move, don't just wait,
For someone else to say,
It's really worth the effort, you'll bless the very day,
So come on now, get on the phone,
Enjoy your friends and share your home,
Somehow you'll never be alone.

Eileen Southey (West Molesey)

With Bunnies And Bounce

May the world be colourful and sprite
And may the passions of love unite
Let your hair down and feel the spring
Where your soul is a place
Beyond the pigs on a wing
Happy be your day in this life
As a time for living without strife
And left for the lover to take you to bed
For bunnies to roam and fill up your head
With fluff, chocolate and ears
Little chicks and the sweetest Bambi deer
So your darling says more from the heart
Never to miss and again fall apart
Never broken or chained by a bond
Of something aching beyond love that's fond
Then to you with a kiss never made
Have a happy Easter as happy is laid
And a lottery is won and the winnings paid.

Anthony Rosato (Surbiton)

Listen To The Trees

If trees could talk, I wonder, would they let us know
Of promises made by loving couples, from so long ago?
Under the spreading chestnut tree, what secrets it could tell
How Johnny said to Mary, that he would love her well.
He'd cut initials in its bark and set them in a heart
So all the world would know, they would never part.
The oak that stands on Richmond Hill, surely would have seen,
Turner in his glory, sketching that great scene.
The linden tree could well be proud to think,
That its sweet flowers could make so good a drink
For those at home and across the sea
Depend upon this lime flower tea
To bring them sleep at night
Far better than the alcohol, that only made them tight.
Has the willow at the water's edge got the least idea,
That its future could well be at 'Lords' hitting balls into the air?

Herdis Churchill (Coulsdon)

Lavender Fields Of Carshalton

Adrift in a lavender sea
So entranced by the heavenly sight
I wander as if in a dream
My senses have all taken flight.

Nectar-drunk bees lazily flit
Thru' an endless field of flowers
Oozing a murm'rous contentment
Of a life full of sun-drenched hours.

While around me butterflies dance
All along the flowery way
In and out of the open blooms
On this glorious perfumed day.

For soon it will be harvest time
And all will come together
People with armfuls of fragrance
In lovely lavender weather.

They know our beautiful flower
Will become many pretty things
Brimful of nature's own essence
And the tranquility it brings.

Daphne Lodge (Carshalton)

Self-Indulgent

I am in a circle, I am going around
My weight is rising by the pound
The reason is easy, rest assured
I stay indoors and get quite bored
And when I am bored, I get to eating
Which in itself, is quite defeating
On top of this to be precise
I don't go out and exercise.

Debbie Lucas (Mitcham)

Holiday In Surrey

I'm in the loveliest of rooms
Surrounded by such sweet perfumes
The smell of coffee at arm's length
A delicious sweet biscuit to give me strength.

Yes, the country house life is for me
Unless I'm stung by wasp or bee!
No, I don't think that will happen
They are busy with flowers and pollen.

I offer to help but there's nothing to do
Except relax as I'm told to do
But soon I will go up and change
I'll choose a skirt from the latest range.

It was at Oxfam that I chose to shop
I find it impossible not to stop
I hope our friends across the sea
Will one day enjoy such prosperity.

But the G8 talks must come alive
Though my V8 still rumbles in the drive!
I must be careful of this resource
Petrol I think will drive the course.

Barbara Tozer (Caterham)

Entente Cordiale

'I'd love to go to France,' I said
The year before the war.
I went and came back full of it,
And people that I saw.

Fifty years on I went again,
This time with spouse in tow
And met my French friend and her man -
Their welcome made us glow.

I've just re-read a note from her
Now we've both lost our men -
That makes it very clear to me
How it was 'way back when'.

'We had to flee the foe,' she wrote,
'Keep just one step ahead,
My brother at the steering wheel,
Or we'd all end up dead.

We'd no spare food or clothes with us,
We drove while bombers dived,
We reached our loving friends at last
And, by God's grace, survived.

After each setback we'd repeat
'It's not the worst' once more
And every time kept going
Till there was no more war.

Just twenty miles of water, then,
A little strip of sea:
Without it we might well have been
Brought low, my folk and me.

'Bravo, la France!' we say again,
Who never really knew
How truly bad it was for them
What they had all been through.

Janet Bowerman (Burnham-on-Sea)

My New Toy

I've just brought myself a brand new toy today
And I've got plenty of time to sit with it and play
But I've got to learn about things called modems and a CD Rom
Before I become full fledge and can have my own UK.Com.

Broadband, Windows, it's all very new to me
I know how to use one of those, is that a recycling bin I see?
Software, hardware and there's such a thing as a Ram
Now in my day I always thought that was what fathered a lamb.

I have to set myself up with an ISP first
Then a PIA before I can go on the Net and surf
And for this a wetsuit I will not need
As at the touch of a button it will come up at high speed!

So I'm sitting here looking at my PC screen
Wondering if I have done the right thing?
I can use my browser all day long,
That's if I can figure out how to log on!

Files insert, format and toolbars
Spreadsheet, database and scrollbar
Ebay, wizard, icons, Internet Explorer
It's like opening a box called Pandora.

But I can take my time you see
And stay up at night until half-past three
Clicking away until I find out what it all means
Even though I'm an OAP and not in my *teens!*

Sue Dancey (Weston-Super-Mare)

The Tree By The Wall

In my garden
By the wall
Stands a tree
Stately and tall.
In spring my tree
Is blossom-decked
And home for many birds,
Late summer sun
Thro' leaves reflects
Too beautiful for words.
But winter leaves
The branches bare
Beaten with wind and rain,
Oh, how I wish
That spring was here
And blossoms there again.

Doris Mary Miller (Wellington)

A Place To Visit In Somerset

Let's take a short drive to Stolford Beach
Away from the hustle and bustle of everyone's reach.
It's now eight-thirty and what a treat
Tranquillity describes Stolford Beach.
It's so quiet you can hear a dropping pin
Just sit and listen to the waves rush in.
The wind's blowing gently on your face
Sure enough, this is the right place.
Take a good look across the sea
There in the distance bright lights twinkle for us to see.
Listen to a neighbour's peacock calling
Now that night-time is falling.
Yes, the winds are very cooling for thee
There's so much freedom, there's lots to see.

C M A Hughes (Bridgwater)

Just Another Smoke

Now to relax and watch the telly
With feet up and a cup of tea.
Ashtray, lighter, packet of fags
Just the ideal situation for me!
So sucking on my cigarette
Then bodging out smoke
Think I'm having a real good time
But my filthy habit's past a joke!

Sitting in my man-made cloud
Of course, don't stop at having one.
The smoke is spoiling everything
Don't worry, think I'm having my fun!
Then as everything changes colour,
Also is impregnated with the smell.
Even washing doesn't remove it
Is happiness really living in Hell?

So one says this is the last packet,
But you know you'll buy another one
For giving up is far from easy, but
Just look at all the damage it's done!
It's no wonder smokers are an outcast
Who wants all this mess in their home?
So just another smoke is not the answer
If you smoke, you'll be out on your own!

Ann Beard (Bridgwater)

Life Begins At . . .

Twenty-two and I have no life to speak of
This hollow of a home ruled
By domineering parents; my spirit
An empty shell of who I am.

Now is the chance
To break free from this existence
The haunting thought
Flows through my mind,
Never knowing what is to come
I will not stay here one second more.

The scary concepts of leaving behind
The places, the faces you know
Is this really the right thing?
Subside as time goes on.

Life should be more
More than a village home
More than a commonplace job.
Around the corner awaits the world,
The future
        My adventure
This is where my life begins!

Nikki Rogers (Bridgwater)

Between Worlds

(In honour of our ghostly lady at 'Downside House' East Hendred, Oxfordshire, my place of work)

Dancing
To a timeless melody
She flits
Across a misty
Dew-kissed lawn
Making
No sound, leaving
No footprints
Long golden tresses
Swirling
Like sunbeams dancing
On water
How long will she
Dance
Through the misty dawn?
Maybe
For eternity
While she is trapped
Between
This world and
The next.

Marisa Greenaway (Steventon)

Ode To Banbury

Our 'sleepy market town's' been shook awake:
Kicking and screaming into conformity . . .
Our 'Banburyness' is being sneaked away
Yet no one seems to care - but you and me!

Our built heritage is vanishing -
Week by unchecked week things disappear
'The Old Cop Shop'; and Spencer House - bulldozed!
And what, we wonder, will be gone next year?

It doesn't have to be a building, either . . .
A few neat stalls, resplendent with their wares,
Can disappear from view in just a weekend
Since privatisation came, and yet who cares?

Our shops now look the same as 'anywhere'
With national chain stores taking up our space
'The personal touch' has vanished (such a shame)
They don't know you from 'Adam' - not your name
And not your face!

Hannah Yates (Banbury)

A Cumnor Tale

It was about two hundred years ago
That he was born
He grew into a man with knowledge
Of a country life
That now has almost gone

An Oxford student he became
His poems still are read
But, through the years his money dwindled
Leaving him with scarce a penny
To his name

He had to leave the seat of learning
And joined a gypsy band
They taught him many things
And how to get a living
From the land

Day after day he wandered
Over the Cumnor Heights
At night he could be seen by some
With the gypsies
Pursuing their tribal rites

The poet, Matthew Arnold was his name
Came to like their way of life
They taught him many an ancient thing
And of the different worlds there are
Between a gypsy and a king.

Mary McGuigan (Faringdon)

Wonderful Now

Forty grand a year and a job up town
A semi in Surrey, two up and two down.
The sun always shines on my front door
I've got everything that I've been hoping for.

Life, wonderful now, wonderful now
Life is wonderful.

Over Tower Bridge we'll make our way
To the air-conditioned multi-storey workplace.
At five to nine I'll check that all my pens are there
Then rest for four more minutes in my swivel chair.

Life, wonderful now, wonderful now
Life is wonderful.

Today in The Times, interest rates are soaring
I hope I get a rise to pay my mortgage.
Perhaps I could ask James if he would have a word with KJ
God, I hate these trains - the bloody things are always late.

Life, wonderful now, wonderful now
Life is wonderful.

I spoke to James at lunch and didn't seem to know
If money was the best subject to dwell on.
There are rumours in the air that could affect our lives
They say our group is being privatised.

Life, wonderful now, wonderful now
Life is wonderful.

I took my photographs and put them in my case
I've always wanted to escape the rat race.
I shredded what was left of my desk diary
And stole the rubber stamp just to remind me.

Life, wonderful now, wonderful now
Life is wonderful.

They repossessed my house on a rainy Friday
It seemed like a good time to take a holiday.
Now I've been on this weekend break for six years
And I've found out just how wonderful *real* life is.

Life, wonderful now, wonderful now
Life is wonderful. Truly wonderful.

Vanessa Hinkley (Didcot)

A New Town - A First Impression

Bicester is a little town with smaller shops than most
Though now a few bigger ones are mixing with their host
Bicester is a little town with shoppers' wants in mind
It serves their requirement in a manner sweet and kind
Bicester is small and neat with an open heart to all
Visitors and locals are most welcomed there to call
Bicester spreads its rustic charm
And lays its welcome on the mat;
To anyone from anywhere it raises up its hat
We were strangers and felt when first we looked around
Our ostrich heads would be better in the ground
But as we soaked up the atmosphere and took a bolder look
We knew that Bicester really was the finest bait we took.

Royston E Herbert (Bicester)

Spare A Thought

When gale force winds are blowing
What do we do, you and me?
We hurry to our cosy homes
And make a cup of tea
Not so our brave lifeboat men
On call both night and day
Ready and willing no matter when
To face the cruel sea
Battling against the elements
To rescue souls in peril
Ordinary folk like you and me
Someone's husband, someone's son
Unsung heroes every one
So next time you hear the forecast
Telling of rough and stormy weather
When you are safe in your cosy home
Just put your hands together
And say a prayer for these brave men
Who never count the cost
Facing untold danger
To save someone from being lost.

Jean Salmon (Pinner)

Good Vs Evil

Trapped by knowledge
Restricted by tradition
Why do I feel like life is a 007 mission?
To no one but God I will show my submission
A light of good will show you the way
The path of evil may make you sway
On every corner there is temptation
It is evil in the mask of an 'unknown sensation'
What is behind the veiled words of the passers-by?
Are they showing you the way or are they a spy?
What is it that you are waiting for?
Is it a miracle, magic or something more?
Who is it that you can trust?
The male mind is dominated by lust
Why is it so hard to be good
Yet so easy to be bad?
Is it my conscience stopping me?
Making me feel sad?
The light of good will always remain bright
Choose your path carefully
Not everything is in plain sight
I hear whispers telling me to come to the dark side
Who is waiting for me?
In whom am I expected to confide?
Evil is always on the attack
What is it that they have lost and want back?
To let evil consume me it will have to do better than that
Don't be fooled by the welcome mat
My faith will help me walk on the right side
My conscience like the sea, there will always be an incoming tide
The soldiers of evil patrol the Earth
Looking for vulnerable people to give them an evil rebirth
No matter how strong evil, good will always win
You can always get forgiveness for each and every sin
Don't let evil rule your heart
You may have seen a lot but this is only the start
The disease of evil starts to multiply
In every war an innocent is left to die

Why is it that words cannot resolve a dispute?
Instead it is taken to the battlefield with men in an armour suit
When will they see that life is too short to fight
Life is not only about might
When will the prayers of the innocents be heard?
Keep it shaken not stirred.

Farah Ali (Uxbridge)

Now U C Me

I'm tryna do rite n write da way I wana write
if my spellin annoys u dis da way I talk mix it up wit my tx
literature's on my own kinda flex a creative step like a dj on deks
I dj wit pens ball pointers, byros im buyin packs of ten
der not pens 2 lend but 4 my expense, 2 write bout life, family, money
n da endz.
So much competition out der ware will my lyrics take me?
2 a place ware its all fame n fortune?
or will I b lower dan usual?
People, im so sentimental, my speech aint flat English
mostly splang I talk wit, but Mum didnt raise no fool
im professional in contest n a gentleman.

The fing iz I put myself in a world ov my own
sumtimes u gotta follow da rulez, cant b hard like stone
this is me all ova ambitious as I got alot older
cant help but touch learnt dat much
I truly inspire da youth teach em how 2 b tuff
not a beef fing but a sensible focussed patch
let it out in ya poemz or rapz
so no beef no death jus that ladder 2 lifes steps.

This is a basic lil poem simple little rhyme
from me writing is not eazy lyrics r words put 2getha by u or me
I luv 2 do this, can write 2 b ruthless or like q-pid
anyfing, jus *dawks!*

Marvin Nathaniel Dawkins (Harrow)

Why?

Why do birds fly in the sky
When human beings can only try
By paragliding over hills and glen
As I set these thoughts of mine to pen?

Why does Man fight against his brother
Because he is different from another
Wars in the east and wars in the west
Since each believes that he knows best?

Why are there stars in the night sky
Shining so brightly until they die?
The moon controlling the tides on Earth
Which may have formed at the time of her birth.

Why is there night and why is there day?
These are the wonders of nature's way
Sun, rain, hail and snow
The seasons are with us and will never go.

These are the questions which we should ask
But knowing the answers is an awesome task.

Aleemah Yasmin (Stanmore)

Small Wonders

As firmly as a staple, padlocked to a hasp
Fascination mesmerised and held me in its grasp.
The mother ewe was grazing, quite contentedly
Her offspring fiercely clinging, so tenaciously.

This baby lamb was busy suckling the ewe
Though newly born, it knew just what to do.
A marvel to the eye had been unfurled
One of the smaller wonders of the world.

The sun was hanging in a sky of lazy, hazy blue
Birds were cooing in the trees, butterflies just flew.
Other sheep were grazing, nuzzling the ground
Unaware that I was there, or anywhere around.

My gaze took in a pretty scene of near tranquillity
The luscious grass of emerald-green, blissful sanctity.
Hawthorn bushes, sycamores, rugged dry-stone walls
Emerging from the hillside, were tumbling waterfalls.

A rabbit hopped then scurried on, deep into a thicket
Summer noises filled the air, none louder than the cricket.
An idle tractor stood aloof beside the five-bar gate
Abandoned to the elements, no farmer, man or mate.

I took my leave quite stealthily, loathe to disturb the scene
Small matter; to those animals, I simply hadn't been.
My mind was full of wonderment, eyes now opened wide
To nature's minor miracles, I raise my hat with pride.

Stan Taylor (Hillingdon)

Tanned Legs

Tanned legs - I swear they make you slimmer
A bronzed calf here, a brown ankle there
A thigh with a touch of shimmer.
Tanned legs - a delight of summer, a holiday treat
A chance to enjoy the fleshy meat,
That makes life mobile, a place to explore,
Yet when winter arrives, you begin to abhor
Their wobbly presence, their cumbersome frame,
A dislike for one's meat that verges on shame.
Yes, tanned legs. They make you slimmer indeed.

Sophie Greenhalgh (Leytonstone)

The Chav

The Chav from Slough what took a bow
In Vauxhall Corsa bound for Staines
With pumping gas and music played
Graffitied on his windowpanes.

A child white, a child brown
Estate of east or west
In Adidas he preened his prime
In the chippie's Sunday best.

He works for Tesco or the like
But swapped to Oil Shell
When Dylan from the liquor store
Lashed out and stole his belle.

By day he works, by night he chavs
On street corners and Staines' borders
Policing streets of broken glass
In Jihad to promote his class.

So what you does and where you goes
Protect your skull and bleeding nose
From bottle head and punch in face
The chav asserts his holy race.

Rebecca Cukier (Golders Green)

If I Were A Magician

If I were a magician, what would I do?
I ask myself - I don't think I'd paint the world pink or blue
The colour of summer, the colour of spring
Just goes to show a magician has a hand in everything.
Things from the past I'd zap right away
But then, where would I be today?
Left alone with no present, no past
And nothing that lasts.
A world of glitter and gold
But what would happen when I grow old?

A magician's work is hard to do
They make things appear in front of you
Hearts and spades is a game of charades
Rabbit in a box and out it pops.
Flowers and gifts a shifty sight
Now you see it and now you don't.
A wand that magics things and tricks
A welcome sight for the eye to see;
A handkerchief that has no end
Jack-in-the-box, that's your lot.

I'd change the world, the poor and the lame
I'll let them see what a good magician I am
No need to worry, I would say
I'd snap my fingers and the work would be done.
With a wand in my hand I would strike a blow
To a troublesome world I'll take my stand.
I'll have my wand to help those who care
A good magician, that's who I am.

Elane Jackson (Winchmore Hill)

How Frank Died

He gasped, he perished on his own
In a small, grubby council flat.
He did not even have a phone;
His post mounted on the doormat.

Nobody heard his final groan,
Except a hideous slum rat.
He died, as he had lived, alone,
Without a friend to have a chat;

The tears in his coat were not sewn,
On which the local thugs soon spat.
And now his every worn out bone
Will dissolve in time's seething vat;

And the sun is no longer shown,
But darkness comes where he once sat

Upon the bench as rubbish crowded,
And he stared while events heaved past.
His shadow must be bleak and shrouded;
The light came, yet it did not last . . .

And all that he is bubbles, boils
And fades into the urban hate -
A pensioner, his hopes, his toils,
Could not endure on this estate.

He hobbled round, upon a stick,
His each limb like a fragile twig.
And no one cared that he was sick -
Henceforth, the sun cannot be big,

But sinks into a concrete crack,
And its kind glow will not rise back . . .

Zekria Ibrahimi (London)

After The Rain

The clouds are breaking, bringing into view
A beautiful sky of azure blue
The sun, above the horizon will peep
Sending its rays across the pastures deep
Illuminating the colours of flora supreme
Dancing reflections from ripples on a stream.

Raindrops collected from showers gone before
Drip from the trees onto the grass-covered floor
Splashing flowers of yellow, red, blue and white
Spreading a carpet of pure delight
Across a green mantle of patterns and furls
In glint of the sunbeams twinkling like pearls.

Clouds leave the heavens as brighter the sun glows
Breeze getting warmer, stimulating the hedgerows
Birds twitter gaily, as from their nests they fly
Blooms open their petals, perfume wafts on high
Bees look for pollen seeking nectar so sweet
Hosts of others follow, joining in the treat.

Butterflies venture forth, no damp to still their wings
Promenading their beauty, what joy the show brings
A cricket gives song as he chirps in the glade
Watching a grasshopper skip from blade to blade
And a spider runs out, his web to survey
The rain may have damaged it some time during the day.

From under a leaf a caterpillar stirs
Wending his way over leafy curves
And because the rain stops, from anthill below
The inmates emerge in never-ending row
Then snail, safe in shell, puts out horns to test the air
No sense in wandering if there's rain out there.

Rose buds on briar open up to face the sun
Ladybirds stalk silently hunting aphids on the run
Dragonfly skims gracefully over lily pad in the pond
While myriads of midges circle a puddle beyond
And the whole insect world seems to come out to play
In a sunny and warm clime this now lovely day.

William Stannard (Canning Town)

In Praise Of Jove

Silver ribbon river slides through dusky olive grove.
I sit under a spooked, half-full, white moon.
Bat skitters past my ear squeaking like a loon.
On nap-night, rug-pile grass, fire ants rove.
Pick out a razor fly with feathers tipped in mauve.
Bamboo rod whistles out - flies - far as an old dance tune.
Unhinge a warm stone. *Plop*. Imagine it's a rune.
A sly tug, an ancient pull. How I pray to Jove.

Beaming day. Sunday brunch: an oatmeal trout
Big enough for laughter, pleased enough as punch.
Serve with sage butter, bread and river-cold beers.
Family, friends - still more. We all spill out.
White plates and children's eyes wide-open for their lunch.
Freeze-frame this miracle before it disappears.

Fiona Gaunt (Hammersmith)

The Hanging Baskets Of The East End

There were these baskets of blossoms sweet
Of lilacs and cornflowers arranged so neat
With pinks and carnations, beautiful creations
Giving an appearance so complete.

Other baskets hung alongside
Of daffodils and tulips, arranged with pride
Of yellow and gold, oh so bold
Glorious to behold.

With just a few flowers and a little thought
Could make the owner so proud of what they had bought
Hanging over the door of a London flat
One doesn't have to move to the country
To find 'Welcome' on the mat.

For each God-given bloom finds room in one's heart
Combined with the perfume each flower imparts
Be they large or small, God gave them all
To be enjoyed as part of His love.

Irene Hurd (London)

The Moon And The Hibiscus

The hibiscus seduced bees all day long
Their proud silhouettes against the setting sun
Weavers sipped nectar, then burst into song
Their kaleidoscope colours: bold and fun
Bright cumulus clouds softened into blush
The full white Eid moon spanned the changing years
The evening's birds and crickets broke the hush
The beautiful sight quelling New Year's fears
This South Africa, the Rainbow Nation
The dust of Africa is in my blood
As I'm the eleventh generation
Angela from Bengal came here for good
My eight times great-grandmother saw these skies
Through the dark lashes of a slave woman's eyes.

Mary May Robertson (Islington)

The Rolling Hills

I'm surely in love with the rolling hills
With their raging varied colours
Their blue-green or their yellowish-browns
They move my heartstrings, pull them down.

I get on a train going out of town
And out it goes, without the sound
I sit with ease and take my chance
Dressed as the Queen and my feet dance.

The fresh air fills my lungs and I get hungry
Getting out my nibbles and I am bouncy
Looking out of my window, my cows and sheep I see
I'm feeling so good, that's just me.

There I see the ploughed fields and the birds in tow
And the flowers by the trackside where they grow
My train is through the tunnel and out it comes again
My eyes in the distance, the countryside view is here to reign.

The city is too busy, people rush about all the time
Go to the countryside and feel fine
Recharge the old batteries, skip about and feel fresh
Oh look at the trees and grasses, you haven't seen yet.

MS Joseph (Stockwell)

The Tree Of Thoughts

Have you ever wondered by and by
Where do our thoughts go, up in the sky
Or is there a very special place
Where all our thoughts go and stay with grace?

Like my old tree of many a thought
So many views and tears there I've brought
Well, maybe our thoughts they too could grow
Like the tree all things start small you know.

Then, once it starts, it just grows and grows
With knowledge learnt, not everything shows
Some things are dark and some things are light
Some a mystery revealed when right.

Many friends will sit around your tree
With the knowledge of friendship sipping tea
Tears, laughter and many secrets told
To the tree of thoughts who stands so bold.

So as you sit now and wonder why
And if thoughts go up into the sky
It's just a thought, this old tree of mine
It's somewhere to keep our thoughts in line.

Rose Mills (Clapton)

Metropolis

I awake in the morning
To be greeted by sunlight
And as I peer through the window
To the left then to the right,
People, houses and streets
Is the view that I see,
But I wonder if anyone
Will ever notice me?
They just go about their business
In the same routine way,
Drop the kiddies off to school
Then go about their day,
So, I dress and stroll downstairs
And into the garden I go,
Maybe I'll see a neighbour
Who will smile and say hello,
But as usual they stay hidden
Behind their privacy screen,
From day to day and month to month
There's no one to be seen,
I wonder if they're really there
And do they know I exist?
I wonder if I wasn't here
Would my presence be missed?
But that's just the way it is
In the suburbs of the city,
No one wants to share themselves
And it's such a shame and pity,
So, I'll accept my loneliness
Is the way it has to be,
And I'll do the things I do
With my dog for company.

Pauline Jones (Chingford)

May Day In Holland Park

The sun is shining, yellow, warm and bright
The sky is blue, shimmering in sunlight
Birds fly around, peacocks walk in the park
The park is open from morning to dark.

A waterfall flows into a small lake
With goldfish, rocks, stones and statues to make
The leaves of the trees are green, red and brown
People come walking, relaxing in town.

Beautiful flowers, red, pink, white and blue
Plenty to see here and plenty to do
Ecology centre garden to grow
Birds sing and twitter and fly high and low.

Mothers with babies and old people walk
Some read a book, some wander, look and talk.

Susan Mary Robertson (West Kensington)

Trust

It's a thing you win
It's a thing you earn
It's a thing that takes
Time to get
But can be
Broken in a second
It's a thing needed
In any good relationship
Big or small
Friend or boyfriend
It doesn't matter
It's expected in a family
And definitely in a marriage
What is it
Do you know?

Thomas Relf (Ashford)

WWDND

He wouldn't shout or freak you out
He's kind and thoughtful, of that, have no doubt
He wouldn't stray or go behind
What you would see as enemy lines
He opens doors, lets ladies pass
He'll deal with cads, put them on their arse.

Today has been his awakening
From a life that's burnt to Hell
He's loving himself again
Can you not tell?
He's drinking from the cup of nature
He's bringing home the bacon
He's making sure his girl is happy
Of that there is no faking.

'Would one care to dance?' he'll say with delight
You cannot resist his charm, try as you might.
'I'll look after you, you'll see.'
'We'll be fine together, you and me.'
'We'll climb the highest mountain
And sing until we are sore
We'll dance together in the fountain
Like no 'friends' have done before.'

Ladies always come first, to his way of thinking
Now he's got somewhere, there'll be no more drinking
He'll play golf when his lady is busy
He won't ever let her get in a tizzy
Cos then he'd be horrible and that's just not true
I question myself, *What Would David Niven Do?*

Paul Clarkson (Gillingham)

Bubbles

Walking along as confident as can be
Be children playing in the street blowing bubbles free
Free flowing in the air as I was walking under
Under God's house the bubbles burst at the sound of thunder
Thunder had cracked the sky and the bubbles made me wet
Wet I was from bubbles and the rain was not driving yet
Yet I still was confident cos I saw the children laugh
Laugh they made me too in the street until I split in half
Half of me was laughing cos inside I felt like crying
Crying cos my horse called Bubbles fell and was lying
Lying on the floor when she had led the race
Race I bet on Bubbles my only saving grace
Grace the children prayed when I told them about Bubbles
Bubbles, please dear horse, go to Heaven with no troubles
Troubles I had known before I lost my life and house
House the children played outside belonged to my spouse
Spouse who used to fly as confident as can be
Be children playing in the street blowing bubbles free
Free flowing bubbles of hiccups I had popped on beer
Beer led me to marry a horse an ugly mare you'd fear
Fear I felt as she was leading my race of life dear Bubbles
Bubbles my wife, I'd bet on always caused troubles
Troubles she'd always cause me, she'd always lead the race
Race of the racetrack and onto the street face
Face of children laughing at my stupid mare
Mare they would make wet when bubbles burst in the air
Air that I breathed now I was crying my heart bare
Bare tears of laughter did the children at Bubbles my driving force
Force they laughed at when I said I married a crazy horse
Horse named Bubbles and the bubbles children blew
Blew my life on Bubbles if only the children knew.

John Lee (Whitstable)

Oh How The Other Half Live

If through the years you are quick enough
And keep your ears near to the ground
You will find it quite amusing
Listening to other folk around
A man went home to wifey
Quite late and worse for wear
So the lovely dinner was thrown
And landed in his hair
Standing his ground he spoke
Not really caring a toss
So she threw a saucepan straight away
Just to show who was the boss
Next day he was just the same
It was like talking to a log
So keeping her cool she calmly said,
'Your dinner is in the dog.'

Daphne Fryer (Canterbury)

No Vices (Not Anymore)

These days I have no vices
I resist eating ices
I've given up smoking
And it's seldom that alcohol
Passes my lips
But still all the weight
Goes on my hips.
Sex is only in my imagination
And it's highly unlikely I'll meet
The man of my dreams.
Just someone to be with
Who is what he seems!
Someone to laugh with, to cuddle
And kiss
A man I can care for is all that
I wish.

Elizabeth Morton (Hythe)

The Stream

Five and twenty miles from London Town
Lies Eynesford, the best kept village for miles around
There you will find ruins of a castle old
And ancient church with steeple bold
There's many a pub with welcome sign
But off the cuff Five Bells comes to mind
We saw long-haired cattle grazing along the way
To the Roman ruins where we walked one day.

A stream runs through its beginning and end
To which droves of people with children tend
They all come from miles around
To net the tiddlers to be found
In that crystal water, crystal clear
Cascading through waterways far and near
How many eyes have looked before
Down in the depths of the river's floor?

To be mesmerised as it flows so free
Taken back in time and the life that used to be
It is relentless in its rush
Its magical sounds the world seems to hush
I felt like I would like to be part of this moment
Submerged and immersed away from life's torment
To be wildly frantic, twisting and turning
To be endless, timeless, free from the yearning.

To feel the earth solid below
The blue skies soaring above as I flow
Onward forever each moment a joy
Abandoned, unstoppable, no time to be coy
So soothing and tranquil, the surface like glass
The regal swans glide along in a mass
Whilst ducks dip their beaks below in the mire
I lie on the grassy banks, there I retire.

Shaded by willow trees draped to the ground
My heart beats in time to life's throbbing sound
Here in this village the church bells chime
The day's drawing in as the clock strikes nine
The train rattles through its part of the scene
And life goes on much as its ever been
One last look across the field to its arches
And back to the present, how time marches.

Jacqueline Oung (Sevenoaks)

That's Life

Sitting, waiting, staring
At the TV screen
Hoping you'll soon be a millionaire
Do you know what I mean?

Each week now I do this
I'm going to win, I know the signs
Each of the numbers before have come out
But they were all on different lines!

Why does this always happen
I guess I may have a collection of three
But why can't the jackpot winner
Eventually be me?

I have got to brace myself
For this week it's me for sure
In fifteen minutes I just know
I'll be jumping up and down on the floor.

But will these be jumps of joy
Or disgruntled leaps of dismay?
Well, I dare say whatever it is
I'll live to see another day.

And that's all that really matters
Your health that has no price
But I dare say I'm not the only one
Thinking the jackpot win would be nice.

Marvyn Attwell (Ramsgate)

Changes

Houses, great red-brick estates
With no boundary fencing or gates
Modern homes with smaller windowpanes
Conforming to these heat conservation days
Utilising all existing land and former country lanes
Seemingly built at angles in most peculiar ways
Buildings, viewed from sideways on
Brick arch-shaped windows echo the past
Resembling chapels of days now long gone
Aloft the television aerial mast
Heavenwards directed high
Modern day cross; vastly changed in form
Today, I realise upon a sigh
That materialistic worship seems the norm.

Betty Bukall (Ashford)

Lost Our Way

There are times when we all feel alone
Lost our direction, not sure where or which way to go
Struggling with an addiction, affliction or maybe
Our own conflictions.

Have faith and the bad times will fade
Mistakes we have all done and made
Follow your intuition and it will lead you on the right path
Use your imagination, its areas are so vast.

We all have hunches as to what is right and wrong
Reminisce on the good times and don't dwell on the past
Time heals bad memories and helps us to grow
The experience to others we can to them show.

After we have suffered true pain
We have nothing to lose and everything to gain
Your heart grows bigger and you really begin to share
A universal love is transmitted into the air.

Have your dreams but never forget
Treat others like you would like to be treated yourself
Self respect you can learn
But other's respect you must earn.

A kind word, a tender touch
Costs you nothing and means so much
When a person feels alone and has lost their way
A listening ear and compassion can help make their day.

Catherine Keepin (Gravesend)

Where We Live

Whilst we are in the countryside we never feel the need
To think about anything to do
With the busy strains of life
Connected to the city or town we may have left
Just glad we are away from the strife.

The scenes around us are part of our need
To forget the worries of everyday life we lead
Different colours enter our minds
As we look and search for glorified signs.

Widespread fields with growing seeds
Supply our minds to achieve
Soul renewed and body tunes
Grateful for this wonderful mood.

We cannot be aware that time is on its way
This is why we must make the most
Of where we live each day
Be it in the countryside or even on the coast.

Iris Crew (Rochester)

Another Class

Not so very far from here,
Young folk lived importantly,
Thinking better without darts and beer
They aspired high to scone and tea.
For in this life it's up and go
Without a mingling trouble,
Drifting agog where fresh winds blow
Which lash, harass or burst in bubble.
Staggering on a pavement, is not refined or tame,
Boys cycling to and fro on footpaths
Shouting, slipping sideways, thinking it's a game.
Until discipline shows its wrath
So it's bucket, spade and seaside
To the beach with candyfloss
Large pebbles and crab at Brighton
Where horses' bets are lost.

Tom Cabin (Beckenham)

My Friend, Phyllis Remington

I am so very sorry, Phyl
Your note on the Queen Elizabeth was wonderful
I never got back to you
So much to do, felt so awful

From working together in Lincoln's Inn
So long ago
Lyons Corner House in
Chancery Lane
Before Hitler, so serene

Later at the Stationery Office
Counting friends as they arrived to work
Each day, sleepless nights
Hoping everyone is all right
After bombings all night
Outings on our days in lieu
VE Day
Everybody going their separate way.

Phyllis O'Connell Hampson (Bromley)

Mid-Life Crisis

I woke up one morning all perky and bright
Then suddenly felt that all was not right
I ponder a while, then quick as a flash
Think, *yes, tonight is my big birthday bash.*
You know, of course, which one I mean
The dreaded '50' and I'm not very keen
Now yesterday's gone, I was feeling just fine
But then, of course, I was forty-nine.
I don't think I'll bother to get out of bed
I've so many notions going round in my head
Will I be able to cope now it's here?
That is the thing that I most fear
Shall I get up and start a new job
Or mope around here like a big fat slob?
You tell me as you've have your '50'
I suppose you will say, yes, have a go!

Vera Hobbs (Dartford)

Crazy Paving In The Garden

Willow trees weeping over Dutch barn
Narrow lanes, real countryside stitching the yarn
Numerous roundabouts, stopping to ask
Was this the right route, what a task
Amber lights glowing like a Turner dawn
Shake up lazybones, do not yawn
So many appeared to know the route
Lucky we did not end up in Beirut
We didn't require Whitstable Bay
It was far out of our way
Eventually an old chap gave the right code
We fetched our vessel in the right road
Crunching on pebbles, bones on bed
Just the right style for a shot I said
Clicking and clacking, my spine almost done
I shaded my eyes to look at the sun
Flocks of pigeons curling in the air
Nothing after all for us there
We came back in the fast lane
Only too glad we had seen it - driving insane
Looked to the left - billowing sea
Glad it was home and back to tea
Try Herne Bay at your peril I thought
Westgate was known - now I'm not fraught.

Joy Sheridan (Westgate-on-Sea)

Ned

I am cat, look at me
Leaping around the garden
Running up the tree
Playing in the long grass
I've covered myself in burrs
But everyone around can tell I'm happy
They all can hear me purr
For I am cat

Butterflies and hedgerows
Nettles and bees
Cleaning my paws, toes outstretched
Under the magnolia tree
I am cat
Stalking mice and creeping around
Lowering my body flat to the ground
Catching the birds
For I am cat

I am cat, watch me go
Running and jumping
Out in the snow
It's cold outside
So inside I go
The children are sleeping
The fire aglow
Home is where I am best off
I know
For I am cat.

Jane Cooter (Gravesend)

The Ups And Downs Of Macular Degeneration

On the pine table there was a crumb
I tried to pick it up with finger and thumb.
I can't understand why I am unable,
'Cos, Nanny, it's the pattern on the table.'

On the bathroom carpet there was something black
So with my slipper I gave it a mighty whack
With a wet tissue I picked up the stuff
Only to find, I had slaughtered a bit of fluff.

There was a mark on my forehead
I scrubbed it until it hurt
My family laughed and said,
'Mum, it's a cut, not a bit of dirt.'

The downside of my diminishing sight
Is I don't recognise family or friend
If they have their back to the light
They could be black, white, or a faceless fiend.

The expression 'As blind as a bat'
Aptly describes me when it's night.
The world is a grey/black blob
I can only see if there is light.

But life's not so bad, I still manage alone
My house lit up like a Christmas tree
I do my garden, decorate, cook and clean my home
The results of my efforts would be nice to see.

Lynne Walden (Gravesend)

The Seal

A little seal was playing
One day upon the ice
Oh, he thought, and full of fun,
Isn't this so nice?
Along there came a hunter
With his hakapik
And hit him all across the head
To skin him double quick.
Alas, the seal was conscious
And scrambled for his life
But nothing he could do
Prepared him for the knife.
His tiny form lay bleeding
But his soul was free to roam
To the arms of loving Christ
Who called his ice child home.
Then does that Jesus Christ
Regard His manchild grim -
A baleful, greedy soul -
And think, *I died for him.*

Iris Pyves (Bexleyheath)

At The Airport

If like me you like to people watch, I know a perfect place to go
Come along to any airport and mix with the crowds hurrying to and fro.
I sat and watched two grown men as they played fast track
They entertained me for a while, playing excitedly
As two schoolboys, I couldn't help a smile
As each one became the victor, they broke into a moonwalk dance
Looking over their shoulders hoping for an audience by chance.
Now look around you, spot the seasoned travellers
Dressed for comfort, not for show
Their battered luggage begs the question, how much further can it go?
They're so accustomed to the waiting game at airports
They can settle down in any space
Laying their heads on faded holdalls,
Arms and legs wrapped round their case.
In sharp contrast are the 'airport virgins' among the crowds
They stand out a mile
Dressed up for their exciting journey
With designer luggage in the latest style.
Be careful not to bump the parting lovers who frequently stop
For yet another embrace
As the saying goes, 'parting is such sweet sorrow'
And it shows upon their face.
In a noisy rush come the last minute travellers
Racing through with jumbled luggage in tow
Hastily searching for the appropriate papers,
Will they make it? You never know.
So next time you are at the airport and you have time to spare
Before you fly away, sit back, relax and look around you
Observe the human race on display.

Eileen Wilby (Chatham)

Park Bench In London

Grease-riddled paper I taste
In the air the smoky fish smell
Famed bus of red in no haste
Destination? Never can tell

Echoes to the unknown spectator
Afar the calling of bells
On the stand catch the front of a newspaper
Conveyor of unwanted tales

Into windows eyes looking to find
A climate more subtle than this
And the leaves have been left behind
By a man with an ache in his wrist

On titbits beaks probe with greed
For this comfort they're happy to stay
Around signs that read *Do Not Feed*
Alas, people know better, don't they?

Well-fragranced lady sits down
Or maybe an ill-fragranced boy
In unison our hands feed the clown
Tears fake? Reflect sorrow or joy

In urgence, in pain, cries a siren
Noticed not by the madding crowd
And the gates, faded paint, rusted iron
That once stood so stocky, so proud

All angles, flash, flash from the cameras
Urban view through a mystified lens
A dustcart is stood where the tram was
And *click, click,* go the fingers again

The faceless charade of the faces
Each one, a book to be read
Obscured in the nearness of places
And I watch while these thoughts taint my head.

Paul Samuel Isaacs (Gyermely, Hungary)

The Raiders

I have heard the wail of sirens
And the ack-ack in the sky
I have heard the falling shrapnel
As metal feet passing by;
Heard the dull exploding bomb
Felt the distant heartfelt cry.

Then I learnt the trick of knowing
When the robot would cut out
And the inborn art of dodging
From a flying bomb's quick rout';
Then felt that heavy silence
Broken by the warden's shout.

Then came a new ugly feeling
The terrorist's hidden fear
A shock blast at Olympia
Suddenly exploding near;
Static exhibits became
An astonished wide-eyed tear.

Alan Dickson (Rochester)

This England

This England, a varied landscape
Fashioned in its own style
Here we can rest a while
Listen to an historic past
'Garden of England' springs to mind
During the war when everyone was kind
With a British Empire firm as the setting sun
Now where has it all gone?

Over the horizon and out of sight?
Everyone doing what they think is right
Historic dramas a thing of the past
Only to see the same dramas cast
On innocent victims of wars that never stop
The remnants of army
No matter if they are out of sight
And softly we sigh for bygone days.

The power of music to hit the breast
The wind in the trees echoes our sighs
And the tears in our eyes.
No time for bureaucrats to think it through,
'Do as I say, not as I do'
In its place violence and crime, less trust
New-fangled memoirs that hit the dust
And the sky gets darker with global headlines
In beautiful Britain where courage will not rust
Till over the horizon at last
Some day this England will rise out of the storm
And England will carry a crown that is not torn.

Joan Hands (Sevenoaks)

The Fishermen Of St Mary's Bay

They are out in all weather, rain, sleet or snow
Quite what the attraction is, I'll never know.

All dressed alike in their waterproof suits
Balaclava helmets and wellington boots.

They set up their rods all in a row
Then stand about waiting for the first fish to show.

They talk about bait, squid, wragworms or lug
While watching their rods for sign of a tug.

They reel it in quickly, what will it bring?
Whiting, flounder or dab, more likely rockling.

They discuss their tackle and tying a good knot
Or there is always the fish that they nearly got.

A marvellous fish, daring and bold
That grows every time his story is told.
As the tide goes out, the day's fishing done
They all return home like the prodigal son.

They moan and groan but one thing for sure
The very next day they'll be back for more.

Christine Collins (Romney Marsh)

An Isle Of Wight Bay In Early Summer

I sit all alone on the seashore
As I've done so many times before.
It's a glorious day in a deserted bay
Here on the coast of the Isle of Wight.

Sun is reflected on shimmering sea
Sky of azure blue forms a canopy
Not a cloud to be seen, just a hazy sheen
Artists long for this quality of light.

The gentle waves of the incoming tide
Wash stones and rocks which cannot hide
From the water's flow, full of life below
Which I cannot see - a myriad species hidden from me.

The water caresses and kisses the sand
As it gurgles in towards the land
A gull on the wing cries overhead
Away from the flock by something he's been led
As he goes out to scavenge the sea.

Here by myself with nothing to hinder me
There's no place on Earth I'd rather be
In this secret cove, known by just a few
I sit on a large flat stone and drink in the view
And listen to the water's sigh and the seagull's cry.

I feel the soft sand between my bare toes
In this lonely spot, not many know
As I swim, the sea is so refreshing
To live near here is such a blessing
I don't deserve nor earn, if to find it I should try.

I linger as the sun sinks in the western sky
And marvel how the time can fly
The sun moves on to wake those in other lands
Propelled by a clock that has no hands
As our day closes the sea gently murmurs still:
'Come to me again another day - I know you will.'

Jackie Hamblin (Isle of Wight)

Lake Isle Of Wight

This place called Lake you can't mistake
Because it's got a station
Otherwise for your eyes' sake
It seems no destination.

Lake is there, remain aware
Between Shanklin and Sandown
It has a council, but no mayor
And this story to hand down.

Lake used to be a postcard joke
'Lake where there is no water',
But that's untrue, do not fun-poke,
It's sea and bricks and mortar.

In newbuild homes with bay views now
Live we of seen isle age;
Seen isle, seen life, seen love, seen how
Faith with forgiveness says, *'Wow!'*

Kenneth Lane (Isle of Wight)

Anchor On The Head

An anchor was dropped on my head last night
It drags behind me as I walk
My eyes don't connect, my vision's blurred
And I feel dizzy as I talk.

In ten minutes time I'll reach my class
Where a hazard of students await
The bright ones scare me, I know I've failed
So I'll drag my feet until I'm late.

Worse still are the ones who know what it's like
With bloodshot eyes they share my plight
I was up rocking my son to sleep until dawn light
But they were drinking throughout the night.

The daytime we seem the same, all stuck in the mud
But every night I'm on duty, whereas they're down the pub.

Sally Sanders (Havant)

The Green, Green Grass

Running across the green, green grass
Landing in the yellow hay
Don't want to let this moment pass
As we sing, roll, dance and play.

People stop to see our games
As we join hands in an old-fashioned way
Reminiscing with pictures displayed in frames
Looking as good yesterday as they do today.

Playing the same games we once played
Having fun in the yellow hay
For I've grown old and time has passed
As I watch you play in the green, green grass.

Gemma Rice (Eastleigh)

From A Penitent Patient

I have upset my lovely Doc, I wrote a naught verse!
I know she wasn't happy and don't want to make things worse.
So now I'll try to make amends, for she's such a lovely girl
With her dark and beautiful flashing eyes
And skin just like a pearl.
So although she didn't slap me, I know that she's upset
And I hope that she'll forgive me, for she's really such a pet.
So this is what I've written for my special visit see
With my favourite little doctor, whom I hope will smile at me.
And that will make me very pleased because I want to see
Her perfect face and happy smile, looking up at me.
So please forgive, oh doctor mine and laugh with me again
And I will promise, lovely one, not to give you further pain.

David Garde (Tadley)

The French Mathematician

Death does not himself harry me
Nor too his dying, with dying ways
As mortals' flesh, so I must flee
But taking too, this dog, his day
As all my histories with me are gone
And shall not retread these steps anew
Though many may upon them, scorn
And question yet, the payment due
As judgements will, and wills be done
Still mine to keep, the value's worth
Not mounting much, yet all but sum
What currency in times rebirth?
Had I but one, that I shall keep
And live forever in this eternal sleep.

Royston Allfrey (Andover)

Bottled Guilt

As bile laps at my tongue
I know it's happened again
The drink has consumed me
The scourge of men
For now I'm simply a puppet
And rage leads the dance
Each verbal bombardment
Each threatening glance.

For those who I care
I now wish them pain
My life so disjointed
Why shouldn't they feel the same.
No logic or reason
Dictates what I say
I just need to hurt them
In the most personal way.

Be it family or lover
I refuse to hold back
The more that I love them
With more spite I attack.
To prey on my loved ones'
Most intimate fears
There will be no mercy
I won't stop till there's tears.

So what is the cure
No vodka, no gin
Sobriety's the cage
That keeps the monster within
But who am I to deny
Its right to exist
It's still part of me
Although it wouldn't be missed.

Without drunken release
Will it gather and grow
Until the beast just consumes me
And destroys all that I know?
Without the restraint
Am I then free to be
The monster I think
People already see.

So herein lies the problem
Who is to blame?
Is my drink alter-ego
Really one and the same?
When so many can drink
And stay angerifree
The beast isn't liquor
The demon is me.

Mathew Jones (Basingstoke)

The Seasons

Icing glitters on the sleeping trees
Wrens huddle close forgetting rivalries.
Underfoot the puddles crunch and break
Now life for many creatures is at stake.
At last this planet tips towards the sun
And trembling buds burst open one by one.
No time to dawdle or to dream
Reproduction is the urgent scheme.
A trillion, trillion births proclaim the spring
Flowers dance, trees rejoice, birds sing.
Even human hearts improve their mood
Soon babes of every kind all plead for food.
Summer comes, the fox lies panting in the shade
The earth is dusty and the flowers fade.
Fruit is swelling on the bending twigs
Apples, berries, apricots and figs.
Human harvesting of fruit and wheat
Means plenty for the mice and birds to eat.
Now is the time to save and store
For winter's winds are hammering at the door.

Daphne Bruce (Lymington)

The Park By The Creek

I watch the evening sun descending on the summer day
 A scent of elderflower
 A squirrel scurries in the bough
 The shadows mark the hour

A knot of boys are bragging over football players and teams
 The park is still adventure
 The paths are endless like the seas
 Life is free - without censure

And bat and ball echo beneath the evening setting sun
 Characters in white languish
 Below the mighty sycamore
 In a land without anguish

And quiet roll the cumulus upon a dainty sky
 The grass is short and browning
 The slumbering creek gently empties
 The poet's faintly frowning

These days are but illusion for the life he needs to lead
 Is passionate yet tender
 And must be passed with one alone
 Both beautiful and slender

I watch the evening sun decrease, suns have no mystery
 Just melancholic sorrow
 The summer comes but always flies
 Will she come on the morrow?

Fraser Hicks (Gosport)

Tanya

My lovely friend Tanya, from Milton Keynes
Loves colours, black, red, blue and greens
Studying for her PHD
She stills find time, to email me!

Mechanical engineering is her field
Learning how to design structures at university in Cranfield
She loves theatres, museums, galleries, films and music
Travelling and helping children, who may be dyslexic.

At 26, and two sisters she adores
One lives in America (Boston) and would like to see her more!
Every weekend she sees her parents . . .
In London, enjoys being given the 'special (caring) treatment'!

She recently bought a house, which is very great . . .
And can't wait till she graduates!
So 'eat your heart out' Isambard Kingdom Brunel
With top grades and with delight, Tanya will shortly yell!

Barry Ryan (Winchester)

Village Joys

Living in my village can be lots of fun
There is so much to do for everyone
The annual flower festival for all to show their skill
To win one of the various classes gives one a thrill
In the summer the charity bicycle ride takes place
Young and old and in-between cycle at their pace
Each year the carnival parade is a colourful show
Round the village then back to the centre they go
Singing carols round the tree at Christmas time
With hot chestnuts, mulled wine and eats of many kinds
And Santa is in charge of the village brass band
With our raised voices we can be heard all over the land
Our new community hall, it sparkles like a dream
Within plays and shows throughout the year can be seen
If from your town life you feel you could flee
Try our village life and you can sing round our tree.

Leonard Butler (Liphook)

Believe

In the twilight of my years
I reminisce with falling tears
Of those I loved, now sadly gone
For those remaining, love so strong!
Age matters not, I have no fear
Those out of reach, I hold so dear.
Love lingers, tempting endlessly
Eternal love, no breaking free!
I have endured three score and ten
Heaven draws near, I know not when
So on the day that I shall die
Remember me, but do not cry.
The promised land is where I'll be
Consider me, across the sea
My heart I leave with those I love
And take my place in Heaven above.
Just think of me and I'll be there
In spirit, standing near your chair
Now close your eyes, believe, believe
It's really me that you'll perceive!

T G Bloodworth (Dursley)

My Village

How times have changed in my village
Everyone knew everyone else
Cottages full of people
Friendliness would always be felt.

No bobby walks up and down
He has gone to pastures new
No longer can you count on him
To tell you what to do.

The cottages stand empty
No friendly face looks out
For strangers now have bought them
For a holiday hideout.

Certainly times have changed
No walking down the village street
Strangers walk along the path
No friends for us to greet.

O Stringer (Bibury)

The Old Dram Road

It isn't working now, of course, no rails, no drams, no horse;
The stream is dry, the wall has gone, just nettles, brambles, gorse.
The slabs are cracked and tumbled, the iron pins misplaced,
The once worked mines and quarries identified by waste.

Where once grew Forest oak and beech are conifers and larch;
Instead of drams of coal and stone, hikers on the march.
Sometimes a mountain biker comes manoeuvring down the hill,
Twisting round the trunks of trees with high audacious skill.

The valley sides are steep and dark in winter's misty gloom
That wraps around the monument which tells of miners' doom.
We linger there and think of them and the brothers brave who died
In the terrifying darkness from the cold and murky tide.

Yet in the spring and summer when the valley sides are green
And here and there are bluebells and foxgloves to be seen,
When butterflies and bees are out and wildflowers fill each crack,
The old dram road, warmed by the sun, is a lovely Forest track.

Shirley Ford (Colesford)

Thoughts Of Childhood In The Wye Valley

(For my parents Bill and Grace)

Come with me down memory lane
Remember all that we held dear
Mother, father, brother too
The joys of yesteryear.

Holidays - bike rides - lots of fun
Family and friends around
Carnivals - parties, all together
Creating a joyful sound.

Thinking of those long-gone days
Some sad, and happy ones too
Looking back through love and tears
Our thanks belong to you.

It's hard to believe dear Mum and Dad
You are no longer here
I still remember those yesterdays
When you were young and near.

We'll live our lives through each decade
So much to see and do
Always cherishing those memories
That we had shared with you.

Shirley Davis (Littledean)

Morning Dew

I remember the green grass glistening in the morning sunlight
No longer had men dressed in white within our view
Yes, I remember because of that sunny afternoon
That resounded leather on willow on that hot summer day in late June.

I walked, wet turf, my footprint indented in that morning dew
The green glistening dew compressed, the depressed morning hue
Meadowsweet, the green, fresh-cut grass is what I saw
To be no more the community deplored.

Yes, I remember the reflection of that June afternoon
Cucumber sandwiches, tea came so soon
The shrill sound sonnet of the mistle thrush shrilled, startling the air
Whit was past, the day welcomed a lady so fair.

The green grass glistens, no longer glorifying the morning dew
The town reflects on the memory
Of the glistening green grass morning dew
Glorifying the memory and mystifying
The memory of the wet willow that summer day.

Ann Hubbard (St Leonards-on-Sea)

Bubbles

The radiance of a bubble
Is something to behold
Its perfect shape and colours
A fleeting life so bold

A busy road in London
A brick missing in a wall
A steady flow of bubbles
Their beauty shared by all

It might distract the drivers
And though I never heard
The creator of these bubbles
Was probably thought absurd

Could it be a West Ham supporter?
Pretty bubbles in the air
Hardly 'Millais' seated figure
Velvet breeches, curly hair

Whoever brightened up the day
With the orchestrated bubbles
Spouting, showy, soapy suds
Merit reward for their troubles.

L G Peach (Seaford)

A Tonic Sight

Of compliments, there've been a million
For Bexhill's De La Warr Pavilion.
At seventy-two, it still attracts the eye,
All long and low, while others seek the sky.

Reclining on the seafront, it's relaxed.
Too bad, to keep it, residents are taxed!
The art within is often avant-garde.
Indeed, it's said, that some should have been barred.

Who'd think that glass and concrete painted white
Could offer times like these a tonic sight?
And, inside, classy styles of yesteryear
Complete a 'thirties look we still hold dear?

So here's to De La Warr, the pioneer,
Who launched the magic project like a seer.
Long may his welcome building bless our shore
Until some graciousness returns once more.

Allan Bula (Bexhill-on-Sea)

Your Wondrous Love

I feel your love warming the night
As I follow the pathway of your flight
Perfumed love lingers all the while
Your sweetness now a cloudy sea
I hear you whisper lovingly to me
Of the wondrous sights that you can see
My love, I hold you still within these arms of mine
To me the Great One, He was kind
God gave to me your sweetness for a while
You left me with your wondrous smile.

V N King (Hailsham)

A Happy Day

I cannot stop smiling, everything feels different today,
I think some of my insecurities have gone away,
I'm happy and just want to play.

Life will not always be this way,
But I can turn things around today,
Rather than being sad, a place I don't want to stay.

'The world is my oyster' comes to mind,
I've learnt the gentleness of being kind,
With my inner strength, I've shaken off the ties that bind.

Julie Marie Laura Shearing (Poole)

Durweston

A Dorset village so full of hope,
A village where folks truly cope;
A village school of which we're proud,
A village concert with big crowds.

The aged church just stands supreme;
For many folk life is a dream;
The numbers in the school just rise,
New buildings will increase hall size.

The playing field gives fun for all,
A merry-go-round, swings, a slide so tall;
The tennis court gets lots of use,
Thank goodness there is little abuse.

Three shops and post office now long in past,
But village hall is there to last;
Its use is great both near and far,
As wedding venue it is a star.

Allotments thriving, we're glad to say,
A great big change from yesterday;
New fence and track have helped so much,
But effort and spirit gives magic touch.

Dorset's Best Kept Village in Ninety-Two,
The place was clean with lots to do;
Not a scrap of litter could judges find
As they searched village from front to behind.

The Youth Club meets in the village hall,
At the river bridge some large stones fall;
This rural village just prospers and grows,
The newly formed cameo club truly glows.

John Paulley (Durweston)

The Mansion House

The mansion stood abroad a wood,
All bleak and bare and grand
With sweeping greens outspreaded
Where bold chestnuts there do stand
And windows tall and windows small are looking all around
Upon a land most beautiful from parapet to ground.

Thereto I see rich tapestry, the bustles and the braid
A lording gent and his lady and servile man and maid
And feasty fetes on pewter plates, a cloistered crowded throng
With fluted ruffs and powder puffs and saffron, pomp and song.

And sunny days are here always and friends come down from 'town'
The creme-de-la-creme, society, in lavish garb and gown
And jolly japes, champagne and grapes, pince-nez and parasol
Paraded here in gay hubbub . . . until the bugle's call.

Thence darkened skies demoralised, no laughter's in the air
No skip nor skirl 'tween jessamine, grim silence everywhere
No cries nor screams from life's young dreams, no motivated mirth
E'en as the listless dust mites doze, fain weeps the pregnant earth.

The muses vent their one intent with minister'al aid
Whence batons in the drawing room our destiny surveyed -
A thousand men, ten thousand then, and many, many more
In order moved - their signature upon a foreign shore.

They fought the fight, by day, by night and night and day 'top brass' -
Passed to and fro with 'yes' and 'no', fighting their brandy glass
They tracked and mapped, hurrah'd and clapped
And pushed their leadened toys
And when at length, we'd upped and won
Drank, 'one more for the boys'.

The years hath flown, the woodland's grown, a forest splendid thrives
With now bedad, a copter pad, wild jessamine and chives
Where sweeping fronds and geese on ponds
And a deer park is the thing
Whilst over all the house stands tall, and children's play-making.

Derek Haskett-Jones (Beaminster)

Seabather

She sat on the beach
Overlooking the sea
On her own as usual
As she liked it to be.
The sand had been covered
By a million pebbles
Nature's army of
Uncontrollable rebels,
White horses aided them
When the sea rough
And for such an invasion
Survival is tough.

A sandy shore
Is a children's delight
Building sandcastles
Which possibly might,
Withstand white horses
As they go on their way
And join children
In the sand as they play.

So much for sand dunes
Seaweed and crabs,
Creepy-crawlies from
Below which the sea's army has.
The jettisoned goods
That appear on the shore,
The scavenging seagulls
That many do dread
That attack without warning
To steal food to be fed.

She sits on the beach
Overlooking the sea
Because that is how she
Likes it to be.

David R Thomas (Ottery St Mary)

Images Of Devon

Sea - creaming in with clutching fingers
Filling the coves and hidden pools,
Sand - harsh and gritty with salt that lingers
Abrasive and hard between wet toes,
The shock of waves with sea birds riding
On lapping water which ebbs and flows.

Inland - sheep on well-marked pathways
Grazing where shivering grasses blow,
Tor crags rising stark on the skyline
With tumbled scree on the slopes below,
And running bracken thickly growing
To clutch and slow the passing feet,
With gorse and purple heather merging
Where ancient, hidden roadways meet.

See clear sweet water flow in secret
Past lone cairns with names which sing,
Mark great birds who soar in Heaven
Then swoop to Earth on beating wings,
Wander by sun-touched, rock-hung water
With stones where brooding adders lie,
Where translucent dragonflies dart and settle
Adding fragile colour to earth and sky.

Watch ponies graze in biting weather
Cropping grasses stiff with rime,
Cross grey bridges and granite tramways,
Hear faint echoes from the dawn of time,
The moor is vast and clothed in beauty,
And round the shore the deep sea sings,
Past and present mix and mingle,
The unchanging heart at the heart of things.

Doreen Neu (Newton Abbot)

A Secret Place

Grandfather sat by the fireside
Just waiting for spring to arrive
While Grandma sat peacefully reading
The big Bible, her faith to revive.

She now felt old winter receding
And knowing that Grandpa would go
To his secret place in the hedgerow
Where the violets, his favourites, would show.

Then as winter gave way to springtime
The birds sang and the sunshine was good
Grandpa reached for his stick in the corner
And 'made off' down the lane, near the wood.

He wandered past the 'pound' and St Vigors
Past the rectory and 'Bissex's' farm
On down the road to the sound
Of the babbling stream, now reborn.

At one point the stream changed its music
Disappearing as though in delight
As it found its own way to the 'big pond'
In fact it was now out of sight.

Grandpa then found the old rough gate
And expectantly he ambled through
Quickening his steps at the thought of
Fragrant violets to find, white and blue.

As he searched among bracken and old leaves
And what remained of autumn's last fall
He at last found the fruits of his journey
The sweet-scented violets, so small.

He gathered a wee bunch, not greedy
Just a token of love to present
To Grandma, so silently waiting
It was spring and he was content.

Mary Dury (Exeter)

How Soon?

Golden sunlight whispers
Upon the rippling waves
How soon the day will pass
So, darkness then enslaves
My lifeline to all that shines.

Regret cuts deeper
My waste of time and tide
Casting off urges to slumber
From its shroud I hide
As I await daylight on my face.

I know day will follow
Every constant night
How desperate my wait
For the glorious light
That eternally will be my rest.

Sue Meredith (Teignmouth)

After You Dear

I can't go first, what would she do?
Who'll clean the dog mess off of her shoe?
And after gardening please don't remind
Just pick up the pruning and tools left behind

Now the mower's quite heavy and for her just won't start
And as I'm not allowed to plant, I can still play a part
These technical jobs are all my domain
Anything with a ladder like gutter or drain

She's proud I can do these important tasks
Who peels the spuds or carrots, don't ask
Although I can't cook, well not like she can
It's a privilege to wash up, I'm her number one fan

You see it's imperative I'm left behind
And I know they'll be a short note for her Hottentot just to remind
My only concern is after you've left
Will the pain go away now I'm bereft?

Charles Keeble (Barnstaple)

Plymouth Hoe

Plymouth Hoe, shared by many
Loved and pleasured by most
Affording spectacular views
Of Devon and Cornwall's coast.

Who can fail to be impressed by this fantastic sight
With Smeaton's Tower, shining brightly at night
On a clear day you can see the Eddystone light
A warning to shipping of their could-be plight.

Drake's statue and the War Memorial high
Uplifting the glorious dead to the heavenly sky
Ceremonial parades, many activities and, even a fairground too
Golfing and bowls and a cream tea or two.

Look down from the Belvedere
On West Hoe and the harbour below
To Tinside, Rusty Anchor and the Art Deco Lido
Across to Fort Bovlsand and the Mount Batten pier.

The huge cross-channel ferries
Easing their way out of Millbay
Passing Drake's Island on a beautiful day
Transporting your mind to places far away.

The Citadel, the Barbican, so much to see
Tall Ships' races, Yacht races and those who waterski
Plymouth's 'Jewel in the Crown' is
The only place, it is said where you can
Hear the sea and see the 'Sound!'

Anne Roberts (Plymouth)

Sons And Daughters

You called out
Your goodbye
As you went out of the door
See you tonight, only you never did
A mother's smile said it all
As she replied, take care
Come straight home
Only you never did.
A cold shiver ran down her spine
As her pride and joy walked away
And she wondered why
Now she knows and no longer wonders why
Tears fall like rain
As she saw life that was so full of joy
Now oh so still
One bullet was all it took
For life on Earth to end with 30 others
Goodbye sons and daughters
May you now lay in peace with angels
Watching over you
And mothers weep for evermore
Because one bullet came from a sick man's gun.

Julia Holden (Braunton)

M Dot E Dot E Dot K

Multi Economic Electron Kor
That's the name of the folk, who live next door
All look alike, even the kids
'I'm told they're computers,' says my husband Sid
It doesn't seem they've been there long
Yet since they have, so much has gone wrong
Most of the people up our street
Are now out of work, even struggling to eat
A problem *they* don't have, next door
Just the odd can of oil left at their door.

Now Sid, and all the factory chaps
Just sit around helpless, hands clasped in their laps
They once built cars on the factory floor
Now these M.E.E.Ks, turn them out by the score
I don't know why, for there is no one around
To afford those cars piled high in the pound
Even these neighbours, who Sid calls Meeks
Don't need a car, they have jets on their feet.

The shop on the corner closed down today
That big 'superstore' took all their trade
Nobody works there, it's run by one Meek
There are still a few shoppers still working that eat
We're lucky, my old Sid and me
We still have a garden so our food is free
But I worry so much, how will *people* survive?
How will those in the towns and the cities get by?

Now these Meeks build more Meeks
Leaving *people* less work
Even my Sid wears a hi-tech made shirt
We are told it is 'Progress' and 'We must compete'
I suppose they are right, for our neighbours don't sleep
They work round the clock, and never go sick
No lunch breaks or tea breaks, just update their chips
No heating cost needed, for they're metal and cold
Maybe I'm just not with it, and just getting old.

Yet the children now growing seem to ask just like me
Nobody understands you see!
Isn't 'Progress' for *people* to improve *their* lives?
To feel love and laughter and give *people* pride
Those 'things' next door, 'those Meeks' Sid says
'You never hear their kids at play'.
So just to satisfy myself
I fetch a book down off the shelf
To try and find an answer there
And satisfy my own despair
And there it is, in black and white
This book, so old, is always right
Yet surely it cannot be true
For it talks of *people* like me and you
But there it is, the very words
It says that the meek shall inherit the Earth.

Rita Shaw (Bournemouth)

Spring Water Music

I just stood there gazing
Into the wayside stream
The sun shone on the water
The shadows dart and gleam
The murmur of the water
Reaching side to side
Sometimes long and narrow
And then out broad and wide
It sang its song of sorrow
And then it turned to joy
It carried wood and branches
And boats with girls and boys
A hymn that's never-ending
Wondrous notes and lays
To its heavenly maker
It swells its song of praise.

George Camp (South Molton)

Packhorse Bridge

Beside an old bridge arching over a stream
Time had no meaning
Passing like clouds drifting over the hill
Life was a song
Lilting and lingering
Soothing and sweet
Small like the pebbles
I found at my feet.

Beverly Maiden (Bideford)

Dollar Cove

I love this little cove, down by the sea
It is a place very dear to me
Most of the tourists will not find
This secret little cove of mine
A lot of locals do come here
Because it's close to the sea and near
Other little coves around
And there's also good golfing ground
You can ride your horses on the beach
And Poldhu Cove is an arm's reach
With the old Hotel up on the hill
You can retire there now, if you will
You can see out to sea for miles
And listen to the seagulls' cries
Stand on the cliff top and feel the breeze
Or pray in the church in peace on your knees
Go out into the churchyard and read the graves
Or walk on the beach where treasure was saved.

Kim Davies (Helston)

The Village

I remember . . . oh, so well!
A village I once knew -
The village of my childhood . . .
The place in which I grew;
I remember the people
And all my companions . . .
The chapel, the church and the school,
The teachers, the brusque but kindly headmaster
Beneath whose wise and firm rule
We learned to listen . . . to think . . . and to question,
For he stretched our young minds to the full;
And so the busy carefree days rolled on . . .
How swiftly the years seemed to fly!
Until and before we hardly knew
It was time to leave . . . to say goodbye.
Though excited and eager to spread our wings,
I, for one, felt quite sad -
For I was leaving behind
A safe, known world . . .
And the happy childhood, I'd had.
Those halcyon days are now long gone -
The world is much changed
As time has sped on
And I have moved far away,
Whilst the village I knew
And the home I had loved
Would not be the same, now, today -
And I have no wish to see . . .
I would rather remember
And hold in my heart
The way that it once . . . used to be.

Elizabeth Amy Johns (Truro)

Dollar Cove

The surf, the shore, a soft confusion in my mind
The sweep of smooth grey stones creeps down to meet the sea
Each stone a name, each name a face
I choose a stone to hold and place.

Eight thousand miles away this vast Atlantic sea
Corrals the rocky shores of Falkland Islands Sound
It's fallen who to God are known
The Good Book says we're 'living stones'.

Now on this sister shore the ocean sings its lay
Reflections captured where the wild sea holly grows
From sense to faith transforming grief
A natural outlet and relief.

Frances Searle (Helston)

Coming To Cornwall

Where shall we go and what shall we do?
Over the Tamar Bridge to Liskeard and Looe,
Travelling on over Bodmin Moor,
Passing China clay pits, reaching Eden's domed floor;
Now we press on as wonders unfold,
Small inlets steeply cragged and tin mines of old,
Stories untold of Cornwall's drama so bold;
Shall we go on or stay to explore
With our caravan parked on a high cliff shore,
As we run over beach and sand
And linger in gift shops, tidal rivers to scan.
We'll travel to Cornwall nose to tail,
And when we shall arrive there its beauty won't fail,
For rounding ev'ry corner new wonders appear,
Never can we find grandeur more fair.

Ben Henderson Smith (Liskeard)

St Piran

Let's hear it for good old St Piran
who came from the Emerald Isle
He floated across on a millstone
It has to make you smile.

Landed here - in Cornwall
and seemingly camped near the beach
Assembled a band of followers
Who well of him did speak.

The 5th century AD was the period
when from Ireland he did come
Washed-up here on Perran sands
it couldn't have been much fun.

Not, ere long, St Piran set to
build a tiny chapel there
For to preach unto the people
his love of God declare.

But I'll tell you now
how he became, Cornwall's patron saint
of tinners in this land
and just because a fire he lit, out there on the sand.

A black rock that was 'neath the fire
leaked out a hot white liquid
molten tin was what it was
and for sure, this was nothing mystic!

So hence black our flag - that is the rock
the white cross, is the tin
Thus it's down to this gentle giant
how our history did surely begin!

Peter Mahoney (Hayle)

Italia

Sunshine almost every day
Above the vineyards and trees display
Terracotta from its deep earth
Of pots with flowers there's no dearth
Artistic flair lies over all
From buildings grand to houses small
Great architecture soaring high
Against that blue and sunny sky
Peopled with a friendly folk
Full of life and song and talk
Welcoming others to their land
Who have a memorable holiday planned
Its mountains, cities, lakes and coast
All combine to play the host
Some of Earth's pleasures indeed cloy
But Italy's there just to enjoy.

Jo Allen (Bromley)

The Passenger Train

Smoke breaking through the memory of time
Wheels chattering along the Havethwaite line
Corridors with compartments, all with blinds
For sleeping at night or whenever it shines.

On a lake of glass where Heaven is near
And time stands still on Lake Windermere
Windows where leather straps take the strain
With a view from the window on the passenger train.

Arm-rests that fold whenever you lie
With overhead luggage racks up on high
Either side of the mirror, individual lamps
And talk of hinges with Penny Black stamps.

The rhythm of the carriages in regular motion
And the power from the engine of a steam locomotion
Clouds of smoke tasting images of the past
And our childhood memories are back at long last.

Gerard Jones (Plymouth)

Your Life

It's funny how 'life' works out for you and only you.
Where you have to go,
What you have to do, whatever,
It all goes to plan,
And who plans it for you,
Only one person,
You surely know who that is.
Think about it,
It won't be any different,
Any way you look at it,
No one, nobody,
Can change it,
So what will be,
And, has to be,
For only you.

E Holcombe (Bristol)

The Old Wooden Bridge

The stream gently ripples
As the birds sweetly trill
And my thoughts sadly stray
To the old wooden bridge by the mill.

As the years pass by
Memories are planted to fill
My mind and my heart
To the old wooden bridge by the mill.

With no sky or sun of gold
The shadowy landscape makes me chill
As my pale face looks with eyes in pain
To the old wooden bridge by the mill.

It was here I left her all alone
When all was peaceful and all was still
Then I cared not I had hurt her so
On the old wooden bridge by the mill.

If I had my life to live over
I'd beg you to love me again, yet still
To forgive your pain at our parting
At the old wooden bridge, by the mill.

Pamela Sears (Bristol)

Chasing Shadows

When the world's a cold and lonely place
And no one knows you, you're out of place
Wandering through life, just another face
The world screaming past, it's just a race.

To stop and look, to feel again
The sun, the wind, the pouring rain
The fear, the hurt and the searing pain
To stop and shout, I'm here again.

Chasing shadows in my dreams
Stop and listen, my silence screams
Bruised and torn, too weak to bleed
Pain is life or so it seems.

Samantha Seward (Newbury)

The Magic Of Bedtime

The clowns in the picture
Stepped out of their frame
One by one
They silently came

Their clear painted faces
All lovely and bright
With tall pointed hats
Made a wonderful sight

The rocking horse stood
He was big and all black
With a shiny new saddle
And lovely clean tack

He tossed his fine head
And said, 'Look at me'
He cantered around
For the toys to all see

A little toy dog
All fluffy and white
With two little eyes
That shone very bright

She was chasing her tail
And having such fun
With the family asleep
And playtime begun

The little toy spider
Had started to spin
A silvery thread
That was ever so thin

So once that was done
He was ready to start
Gently he played
On his very own harp

The teddy bears next
Cos no one could sleep
They started to sing
And were tapping their feet

The clowns found a trumpet
And started to play
Another one started
To bang on a tray

The horse galloped round
With the dog on his back
The clowns found a hoop
So they all jumped through that

The dolls were awake
And gave a big smile
With this going on
They would dance for a while

Soon the whole room
Was alive with the toys
Singing and dancing
They made quite a noise

The clowns made them laugh
They all clapped with glee
It was a wonderful
Colourful sight to see

This carried on
Till the room became light
So they had to all stop
And then say goodnight

So at bedtime remember
To count all those sheep
So your toys can come out
Go quickly to sleep.

Jennie Aspin (Southampton)

I Remember

I remember, I remember the house where I was born
With birds outside chirping each and every morn
And Mum in her dressing gown making a pot of tea
As Dad goes off to work, whistling merrily.

The windows appeared to lean near the cherry trees
As I listened to the whispering of the springtime breeze
And every day was filled with a family full of love
While all our dreams fitted like a well-worn glove.

In the winter the coal fire blazed in the fireside grate
I would rush home from school not wanting to be late
And sometimes Gran would still be sitting there
Smiling at me lovingly from the brown armchair.

Halcyon days of summer and winters full of snow
My friends and I played hard, forever on the go
Mum was in the kitchen cooking shepherd's pie
For us to eat for dinner beneath the darkened sky.

I remember, I remember happy days gone past
Why is it those cherished days never seem to last?
And our memory does linger with rose-tinted cheer
On when we were young and looked forward to every single year?

Linda Hurdwell (Ascot)

A Rose By Another Name

Whilst placed beneath the friendly bough
The winter-flowering blossom tree
And situated at the garden seat
In shade with sun and not a care
I numbered rose bushes fair
Eleven in all and all complete
With radiant blooms of variant charm
Mischief, Iceberg, Superstar and Ruby,
Uncle Walter, Chinatown, Antique and Harkness
Orange, yellow, scarlet and pastel pink
In all their sizes, small and large
Some in bloom and some in bud
Overblown or on the rise
Some awaiting their demise, the pruner's skill
All was hushed and not a sound
Except the cheerful busy buzz of the bumblebee
Settling here and settling there
Wafting midst the summer air.

Margaret Bennett (Burgess Hill)

My Friend, The Raging Sea

The raging sea interrupted my silent thoughts
Glued to the spot, it was solitude I sought
Defying all in its path, it was truly unrelenting
Shivering in awe, I feared its tormenting
If only I could bridle my stress and send it out to sea
On the back of those waves that soar so mightily
What energy, what power, who can tame its wrath?
I shrieked as it sprayed me giving a free bath
Time stood still, or so it would seem
Is it all real or am I in my own dream?
Startled out of my thinking I was well aware
My troubles had left me, they sailed into thin air
I extol the Creator who designed these mighty seas
I feel I've had a tonic and completely full of ease.

Barbara Jermyn (Gloucester)

Travelling

Now in my 83rd year
I've travelled both far and near
Breathtaking beauty of Isles Caribbean
Black Sea and Red Sea and the Aegean
Portugal, Spain, Cyprus then Greece
Malta and Italy where wonders never cease
Yugoslavia, Algeria, Tunisia, the USA too
Andorra and Luxembourg to mention a few.

But of all these lands south, east and west
I think that Egypt is clearly the best
Dramatic display of a pyramid sunset
- A sight once seen - you'll never forget
The awe-inspiring pharaohs' tombs
The amazing painted temple rooms
- Travel the world, you'll see nothing to equal
The fantastic skills of those ancient people.

David Merrifield (Winchelsea)

Clerk - En - Water

I walked back to my past, with my two girls
Slowly, my childhood, started to uncurl
The path I took was one I've never forgot
Memories of yesteryear came to me, then I laughed a lot.

We walked past the house where my childhood was spent
Up past the 'jail' I showed them where the milk churns went
Round another corner, I stood and took a deep breath in
Some of my childhood was without sin.

Lots to see and lots of chatter too
My childhood memories became so, for my daughters, new
I feel so blessed to share what was rightfully mine
We will share precious moments, all three of us, in time.

We were invited to a farm, the girls' faces beamed bright
To see all the animals, the excitement, in time the moment felt right
We thanked the lady for being kind to us all
Down another lane we went, we were careful not to fall.

Enchanted and magical, for me, it still felt
Watching the girls play in the ford, made any anger inside, melt
I watched them as they laughed and also how they played
Into the water and under the bridge, a flashback to me,
I also wanted to stay.

The sun flashed through the trees, the air was so sweet
Thank you 'spirit' for allowing me to visit here, my memories to meet
Once again I was a little girl, with my girls, I was allowed to be
Through the eyes of my daughters,
At last, 'my child', will be able to see.

Patricia Deakin (Bodmin)

Beautiful Australia

If you enjoy water sports: sailing, surfing, sun, sand and sea
Surfer's Paradise is the fun place to be
Australia has some of the world's most colourful birds,
Parrots, crimson rosella and cockatoos
Animals, koalas, wombats, possums,
Platypus, wallabies and kangaroos.

Captain Cook Memorial Lighthouse at Point Danger used a laser beam
This was the first of its kind in the world to be seen
Sydney shell-like Opera House and harbour, what a sight
Plazas, arcades, glittering night-clubs, cosmopolitan dining all
just right.

The Devil's Marbles, north of Alice Springs on the Stuart Highway
Ayes Rock looms in monolithic majesty out on the plains
Takes your breath away
Have you see the flowers?
Golden wattle, fringed lily, guinea flowers and cranbrook bell
This last flower more like a cactus with white bells edged in red
How it got its name, who can tell.

The Great Barrier Reef with its colourful fish
The golden-tailed chaetadon and zebra angelfish
Such beauty which is seen by few
There are rainforests, mountains, vineyards famous in Hunter Valley
Cattle in peaceful pastoral in Wollomombi,
Sheep grazing near Ballerat
Strange trees like the bottle tree and ghost gum and curtain fig
Looking down the Perisher Valley, snowy mountains, what a view.

Anne Churchward (Tunbridge Wells)

Politics

I promise I will change the world
I promise I will be
The finest man in all the land
As far as you can see
I promise I'll be better than him
I promise I'll be good
Won't do the things the other lot did
Oh no, I never could
I promise I'll give you what you want
I promise I'll be true
Just write it down and send it in
I'll get the best for you
I promise this and that
Just let me into Parliament
It'll never change my plan

Thank you, thank you everyone, for you have let me in
The newest ever government, without a spot of sin

I know I promised quite a lot
I know I promised you
But now I'm here it's rather hard
To do what I'd say I'd do
I know I said I've give you this
I know, I know it's true
Let me stay in this nice job
I'll get them just for you
I know I didn't do that much
I know I took my time
But would you choose that other lot
To take the reins from mine?
I know I've had a real good go
I know you think I'm through
Just give me one more little chance
I'll make it up to you.

Thank you, thank you everyone, you've let me in again
The second term in power will hold slightly less pain

The people know just what they want
They chose us here to lead
But not because we are so good
The other lot are weak
We decide what we will do
They can all obey
Ten years here in government
It means we're here to stay
Let's make them pay for choosing us
Let's hit them where it hurts
The people stick to what they know
That other lot are worse
We'll line our pockets with their cash
We'll be careful to conceal
We'll cheer them up by giving back
The money that we steal

Oh dear, oh dear, we've lost our power, it's all gone badly wrong
That other lot are now in there and all our jobs are gone
Well, we've enjoyed the perks of power and all the other tricks
And after all, no damage done . . . it's only politics.

Russell Barr (Watford)

Three Stages Of A Man's Life

Stage One
There is always a palace in your mother's heart
That palace is called love
That love is the bond
That bond is from birth.

Stage Two
What is love?
Love is for sharing
The love from birth
Is yours to keep forever.

Stage Three
True love is respect
Respect is what you give
And when you give it
Give it and receive it
With thanks.

Amarjit Bhambra (Hayes)

My Garden Companion

Robin, my little friend,
Why are you always alone?
Are you living on your own,
How I look forward to your chirpy call
Loneliness can come to us all
There will always be a welcome here
Robin redbreast have no fear
If you wish you can come inside
And under my roof with me reside.
Thank you for your company
And all the pleasure you have given to me.

Gladys C'Ailceta (Burgess Hill)

Synopsis Into Soliloquy

At sweet sixteen I'd heard so much
About this thing called 'love'
They said it dropped into your life
And gave your world a shove.

Wow - so it did - right on the dot
Suddenly - there was *he*
Telling me I was lovely and
There was no one else but *me!*

He had such dreams of things to be
He swept me off my feet
The thought of seeing him each day
Made my heart skip a beat.

I cherished every hour with him
Though Mother warned me: 'Dear
Don't pick the first man that you find
There's plenty more out there.'

But I didn't want to listen
I thought, *he's the one for me*
Together we will conquer all
Don't worry, Mum, you'll see.

We set off on life's journey in 1962
Eight years since the time we'd met -
And I knew I would stay true.

But fate then somehow took a hand
And rocked our little boat
Our troubles mounted thick and fast
And we couldn't stay afloat.

So the parents I'd abandoned
When first I met my man, said,
'Such is life - now come back home
And we'll help all we can.'

They helped us ride through our first storm
To fight another day
But - I never liked that he could *take*
With so few words to say . . .

Soliloquy

At breakfast time my mother and I
Sat down to eat - 'I don't know why,'
She said to me - 'it seems absurd
You're different somehow (though it's nothing I've heard)'

She confided her thoughts on the man I was with -
Hoped she didn't offend; - just wanted to give
Her motherly view - thought he wasn't for me
And he's certainly 'not the only fish in the sea' . . .

I met my man at sweet sixteen just as I finished school
I fell so hard my mother said
'Oh don't be such a fool. The world is full of men
And so just take a look around
Don't pick the first bad apple that has fallen to the ground'.

But
He loved me and he was my world; her words I did not heed
(If I could turn the clock back - what a different life I'd lead).
So - I 'did my thing' and married him. I did the best I could
I worked two jobs in early days in order that he could
Begin his life in business (which had always been his dream)
Then we'd have lots of money and enjoy life to extreme.

But things went wrong the first time - then the second -
Then the third
We lost our home and lived in rooms and yet, it's quite absurd
That I never did stop loving - never doubted him, you see
And even with three children the rent was down to me.

But I never let him down - was always steadfast, true and loyal;
And (apart from satisfaction), I got nothing for my toil.
I worked a job from 8 till 5 although I had small twins
Cos I always sort of thought *if one keeps at it - then one wins!*
But after twenty-four long years, I'd gone off to work one day
And discovered to my horror that while I was out all day
My husband was adulterous; he'd found a divorcee
Who was living off her 'ex' - and had more time for *mine* than me!

My world just fell about me and I wished I could have died . . .
To think he'd spent our money and of all the times he'd lied!
I packed his case and bade him leave (the lesser of two ills)
I said, 'I hope she'll do the same and like me - pay your bills.

I had *no time* for counselling - I had the rent to pay
I had no time - I had no time . .
And he just walked away.

Inevitably
The sun rose and another day had dawned
And all the pain of loneliness returned
And yet - I didn't know that this might be
The starting of a new philosophy.

Still -
No more dreaming dreams or scheming schemes:
The 'normal life' had split right up the seams.
From hereon in I seemed destined just to be
A lone spectator on life as it ought to be.
Sometimes I thought I'd never laugh again
And sure as Hell I didn't like the game.

Yet
Children huddle closer in a storm, so
In consequence I never felt forlorn.
We learned to value health and simple living
The art of hope when there's just love for giving
I helped them see wealth comes in many guises
Material wealth (perhaps) a lonesome heart disguises?
Contentment at what is - not at 'what might have been'
And *still* - through my children's eyes - the strength to dream.

And since that nightmare, the best times that I'd had
With simple freedom, more good times than bad -
Eventually - the chance for me to simply be a *mum* - and to
Care for my dear parents till Maker they succumbed.
And I never had the worry of the rent to pay, you see
And life got slowly better and (though lonely) - good for me
For although I wasn't rich, I was a happy soul - and *free!*
But
I feared about the future and ambition stirred in me
My daughter flapped her wings and she left our family.

For reasons quite unknown my 'ex' rejected our small twins
(They were only four years old when this tale begins)
He was full of empty promises - but never gave them any time
In consequence of which I gave them twenty years of mine!
(Which is 'what it's all about' - and there is nothing I regret
But
There's a nagging deep inside about the future I will get
Because I haven't got a home and (well - not yet) I have no man
So I thought I'd get a job and try to do the best I can
And then one day - if I worked real hard (before I was too old)
I could get myself a mortgage and not 'stay out in the cold'
(Because 'living on the State' you are a 'have not', and you see
I just got discontented with life's hard reality).

Still - there's a happy ending to this tale of misery
'Cause I still enjoy my freedom and I'm happy as can be
It gave me time to write this rhyme - some inbuilt therapy
Because I felt it was someone else - just *anyone* but *me*.

Edna Sparkes (Banbury)

I Shall Fly With Peter Pan

When Peter Pan says I can fly
His words I shall trust
I shall think of happy thoughts
Or if not he shall sprinkle me with fairy dust

When my thoughts surrender happiness
It feels like I am starting to get wings
I do just what Peter Pan asks me to
And think of joyful things

Peter Pan was always right
When my heart was full of joy
My thoughts just lifted me up to the air
And my happiness no one shall destroy

The journey seemed so short to reach Neverland
As I searched for the second star to the right
Suddenly Mum touched me on my shoulder as I stared out the window
She said, 'Honey, you need to go to bed, it's past midnight.'

Sonila Reka (Chingford)

Anchor Books Information

We hope you have enjoyed reading this book - and that you will continue to enjoy it in the coming years.

If you like reading and writing poetry drop us a line, or give us a call, and we'll send you a free information pack.

Alternatively if you would like to order further copies of this book or any of our other titles, then please give us a call or log onto our website at www.forwardpress.co.uk

Anchor Books Information
Remus House
Coltsfoot Drive
Peterborough
PE2 9JX

(01733) 898102